Down by th

By Charlotte Armajo
Illustrated by Lois Ehlert

ScottForesman

A Division of HarperCollinsPublishers

Down by the swamp
when the wind begins to blow,

the dance begins
when the fireflies glow.

3

Spiders spin
around and around.

4

Grasshoppers jump
up and down.

Butterflies flutter
from side to side.

6

The dance can be seen far and wide. Until . . .

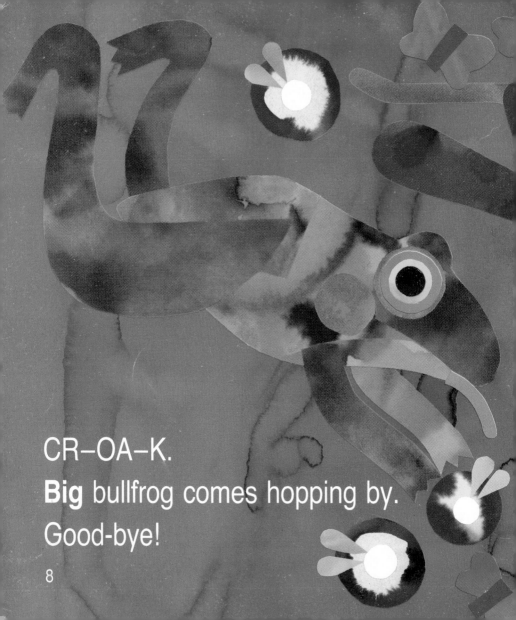

CR–OA–K.
Big bullfrog comes hopping by.
Good-bye!

8